BOOKS BY PHILIP LEVINE

THE MERCY

THE MERCY

POEMS BY

PHILIP LEVINE

ALFRED A. KNOPF   NEW YORK   2000

www.randomhouse.com/knopf/poetry/

My thanks to the editors of the following journals in which these poems appeared:
THE ATLANTIC MONTHLY: "The Return," "The New World" & " 'He Would Never Use One
    Word Where None Would Do' "
THE AMERICAN SCHOLAR: "Night Words" & "Orphans"
BRILLIANT CORNERS: "The Unknowable"
CRAZY HORSE: "I Caught a Glimpse"
DOUBLETAKE: "The Cafe," "Salt and Oil," "Joe Gould's Pen" & "Once"
FIRST OF THE MONTH: "The Unknowable"
FIVE POINTS: "Clouds Above the Above the Sea" & "Sundays with Lungo"
GEORGIA REVIEW: "Reinventing America" & "Northern Motive"
IMAGE: "After Leviticus"
KENYON REVIEW: "And That Night Clifford Died" & "The Three Crows"
MICHIGAN QUARTERLY REVIEW: "Flowering Midnight," "Drum" & "Photography 2"
THE NATION: "Philosophy Lesson" & "After the War"
THE NEW REPUBLIC: "The Search for Lorca's Shadow"
THE NEW VIRGINIA REVIEW: "The Sea We Read About"
THE NEW YORKER: "Little Apple of My Eye," "It Was Autumn" & "The Mercy"
ONTARIO REVIEW: "The Secret"
PLOUGHSHARES: "The Dead"
POETRY: "Smoke," "The Evening Turned Its Back upon Her Words," "Cesare," "The
    Mortal Words of Zweik" & "Black Stone on Top of Nothing"
THE PROGRESSIVE: "The Communist Party"

My thanks to the Bellagio Study and Conference Center where several of these poems
were written.

My thanks to my wife and my friends Peter Everwine and Edward Hirsch; the three
of them helped me with criticism of individual poems as well as with the structure of
this collection.

Library of Congress Cataloging-in-Publication Data
Levine, Philip, 1928-
    The mercy : poems / Philip Levine.—1st ed.
    p.   cm.
    ISBN 0-375-70135-4 (alk. paper).
    I. Title.
PS3562.E9M47   1999   98-43353
811'.54—dc21   CIP

Manufactured in the United States of America
Published March 30, 1999
First paperback edition October 2000

IN MEMORY OF MY MOTHER

ESTHER LEVINE

1904–1998

CONTENTS

I

SMOKE

Can you imagine the air filled with smoke?
It was. The city was vanishing before noon
or was it earlier than that? I can't say because
the light came from nowhere and went nowhere.

This was years ago, before you were born, before
your parents met in a bus station downtown.
She'd come on Friday after work all the way
from Toledo, and he'd dressed in his only suit.

Back then we called this a date, sometimes
a blind date, though they'd written back and forth
for weeks. What actually took place is now lost.
It's become part of the mythology of a family,

the stories told by children around the dinner table.
No, they aren't dead, they're just treated that way,
as objects turned one way and then another
to catch the light, the light overflowing with smoke.

Go back to the beginning, you insist. Why
is the air filled with smoke? Simple. We had work.
Work was something that thrived on fire, that without
fire couldn't catch its breath or hang on for life.

We came out into the morning air, Bernie, Stash,
Williams, and I, it was late March, a new war
was starting up in Asia or closer to home,
one that meant to kill us, but for a moment

the air held still in the gray poplars and elms
undoing their branches. I understood the moon
for the very first time, why it came and went, why
it wasn't there that day to greet the four of us.

Smoke

Before the bus came a small black bird settled
on the curb, fearless or hurt, and turned its beak up
as though questioning the day. "A baby crow,"
someone said. Your father knelt down on the wet cement,

his lunchbox balanced on one knee and stared quietly
for a long time. "A grackle far from home," he said.
One of the four of us mentioned *tenderness,*
a word I wasn't used to, so it wasn't me.

The bus must have arrived. I'm not there today.
The windows were soiled. We swayed this way and that
over the railroad tracks, across Woodward Avenue,
heading west, just like the sun, hidden in smoke.

FLOWERING MIDNIGHT

After the rage of the anvil, the terror
of iron striking iron and iron striking back,
the streets outside Chevy Gear & Axle
overflow with silence as the snow comes down
slowly at first and then whitening the night,
filling the few horse chestnuts with blooms
as full as peonies.
           The bus doesn't come,
the street lights stutter, and in the shadows
two of us stand smoking in silence, glad to be
held by silence. Two men, still young but far
from childhood when we slept through nights like these
to waken to a new world, the lost white world
we thought was ours for good.
                 I grew moss roses
in the little rock garden behind the house
of my growing up. Was that yesterday,
when I was twelve and my hands reeked of dirt
blackened with compost, when the spring battered
the mock orange into blossom, and I dreamed
of flowers like these?
            I knew then the world
would be flowers like these: the blood-red roses
bursting along the fence even into autumn,
the single dahlia brought down by its own weight,
lilies of the valley, cosmos, and beyond
the wild fields of milkweed, flags, the trash dumps
alive with gray rats.
          My friend Marion,
the ex-junkie and novice drop-forge worker,
off by himself humming "Body and Soul,"
stares wide-eyed straight up letting the flakes
fill his mouth. He played with Hawkins before
his troubles and now has four ten-inch Bluebirds
left to prove it. Now even these trees hunger
for the music, three black trees filling with winter.

AFTER LEVITICUS

The seventeen metal huts across the way
from the great factory house seventeen
separate families. Because the slag heaps
burn all day and all night it's never dark,
so as you pick your way home at 2 A.M.
on a Saturday morning near the end
of a long winter you don't need to step
in the black mud even though you're not sober.
You're not drunk either. You're actually filled
with the same joy that comes to a great artist
who's just completed a seminal work,
though the work you've completed is "serf work"
(to use your words), a solid week's worth of it
in the chassis assembly plant number seven.
Even before you washed up and changed your shirt
Maryk invited you for a drink. You sat in the back,
Maryk and his black pal Williams in the front,
as the bottle of Seven Crown passed slowly
from hand to hand, eleven slow circuits
until it was empty and Maryk opened
the driver's side door and placed the dead soldier
carefully bottom-side down on the tarmac
of the parking lot and then drove you home
or as close to home as he could get
without getting his sedan stuck in the ruts.
Neither Maryk nor Williams had made a pass,
neither told a dirty joke or talked dirty.
The two, being serious drinkers, said
almost nothing though both smoked and both sighed
frequently, perhaps from weariness,
from a sense of defeat neither understands,
or more likely because their lungs are going
from bad air and cigarettes. You're nearly home
to number seven, where a single light burns
to welcome you back with your pay envelope
tucked in your shirt pocket, the blue, unironed
denim shirt your oldest, Walter, outgrew

eleven years ago. Bernadette Strempek,
let me enter your story now as you stand
motionless in the shadowy black burning
inhaling the first warm breeze that tells you
this endless winter is ending. Don't go in
just yet; instead gaze upwards toward the stars.
Those tiny diamonds, though almost undone,
have been watching over your house and your kids
while you've been away. Take another breath,
a deeper one and hold the air until you can't.
Do you taste it? You shake your head. It's God's
breath, a magical gift carried
all the dark way from Him to you on the wind
no one can see. Seventeen separate huts
hunkered down and soberly waiting, this night
three of you in a '47 Plymouth four-door
drinking Seven Crown for eleven circuits
until the work was done, one woman alone
beneath the blind sky, standing patiently
before number seven Mud Lane taking
into her blood one gasp after another
of the holy air: the numbers say it all.

DRUM   *Leo's Tool & Die, 1950*

In the early morning before the shop
opens, men standing out in the yard
on pine planks over the umber mud.
The oil drum, squat, brooding, brimmed
with metal scraps, three-armed crosses,
silver shavings whitened with milky oil,
drill bits bitten off. The light diamonds
last night's rain; inside a buzzer purrs.
The overhead door stammers upward
to reveal the scene of our day.
                                        We sit
for lunch on crates before the open door.
Bobeck, the boss's nephew, squats to hug
the overflowing drum, gasps and lifts. Rain
comes down in sheets staining his gun-metal
covert suit. A stake truck sloshes off
as the sun returns through a low sky.
By four the office help has driven off. We
sweep, wash up, punch out, collect outside
for a final smoke. The great door crashes
down at last.
                        In the darkness the scents
of mint, apples, asters. In the darkness
this could be a Carthaginian outpost sent
to guard the waters of the West, those mounds
could be elephants at rest, the acrid half light
the haze of stars striking armor if stars were out.
On the galvanized tin roof the tunes of sudden rain.
The slow light of Friday morning in Michigan,
the one we waited for, shows seven hills
of scraped earth topped with crab grass,
weeds, a black oil drum empty, glistening
at the exact center of the modern world.

ORPHANS

The field mouse in his little gray cape
has been walking the night playground
beside me as I gaze upward at stars
puzzling this way and that. The long day
at last has come to a close; the darkness
rising from the grass sighs with relief,
the quarter moon stumbles out from behind
a ghostly cloud, surveys the scene, and returns.
At just this point a spirit with a name
should settle on my left shoulder to whisper
the night's first great truth, and thus, humbled,
I would respond from deep in my soul.
I stop and listen. I can hear cars
speeding on the nearby streets, a truck
backfire and stall. My own mind backfires.
Sixty years ago a Mrs. Morton
made me kneel beside my bed to pray
that if I died before I woke her god
my soul would take. I had planned to sleep
until morning and wake in sunlight,
but now death, god, and the soul entered
the scheme, according to Mrs. Morton.
"Take my soul?" I asked looking up
into her talcumed face. "Take your soul!"
she repeated, her wet teeth gleaming
with religious light. My two clasped hands,
my knees aching on the bare wood floor,
my eyes closed on my mind's shooting stars,
all these were actual, like the bad breath
of Mrs. Morton, the diamond rings
she wore, the dyed blond hair, snooded,
the gartered thighs I tried never to see.
Thus it was determined in childhood
I would walk on crushed grass this evening
seeking counsel from the quarter moon,
the starry skies in their confusion,
my friend, the somber field mouse, silent,
wise, an orphaned spirit like my own.

THE COMMUNIST PARTY

Seven single, formal men slowly circling
the scarred ping-pong table with its sagging net,
with its bottle of pink Michigan wine,
a plate of stale Saltines, the cheese long gone,
one bruised apple, a soda, and nothing more.
Near Eastside, Detroit, October, '48.
My brother and I looking for girls or women
interested in almost anyone, for we
were almost someones. Forty years down the road
the phrase "sexual politics" would surface
only to die into jargon; that night we
could have used it. I'll spare you the argument
with the one decent girl who called Reuther
a little fascist, the turn-table that ground out
"Petrushka" over and over with a will
of its own, the posters for Henry Wallace,
the plywood square for dancing where two girls
in chinos and sweaters frowned under a bare bulb,
the brick and board bookcase and its virgin copies
of *Das Kapital* and Jack London's novels,
the rain-streaked windows opening on a parking lot.
We stayed forty minutes talking to each other
like a husband and wife in a foreign country
and left with nowhere else to go that night.
We called it experience and laughed it off.
I've partly played this for laughs. It wasn't
that funny. The two of us were looking
for what we couldn't articulate, and so
we said "girls." Were we simply idealists?
What I'm certain of is something essential
was missing from our lives, and it wasn't
in that sad little clubhouse for college kids,
it wasn't in the vague talk, the awful words
that spun their own monotonous music:
"proletariat," "bourgeoisie," "Trotskyist."
Whatever it was we didn't find it there
among a dozen strangers of good will,

we didn't find it there or anywhere.
Perhaps that's why I go back again and
again in my imagination to a night
I could have changed my life or ruined it
or found it for a time. What was missing?
This freezing afternoon in early March
on the downtown 6 headed for Bleecker Street
I read a list of plain words—boots, rack, bin,
box, hose, rake, broom, saw, ax—household words
put down by an Australian novelist
in a book of true stories she'd sent me.
A singular woman who'd created herself
out of the need to be only herself.
Her family names, I thought, reborn on my breath
as I spoke them quietly to everyone.
It's never too late, is it, to lose your life.

AND THAT NIGHT CLIFFORD DIED

We broke for lunch at 8 P.M.,
in my case two sandwiches
of fresh lettuce and Genoa
salami cut so thin the light
shone through the slices when Faso,
the Sicilian butcher, held
them up to boast of his art.
I lived alone in a one-room,
walk-up apartment across
from the Catholic seminary
on Lawton. In the late hours
when I came home on foot from
the street-car stop on Claremont
I could see black-robed men walking
in silence beneath the elms.
I envied them the quiet,
the massive iron gates that kept
the city out, the thick-leafed trees
that caught what faint light there was
and gave it back to the night.
I did not know who to thank
for my life. The radio
softly played gave me music—
my Polish neighbors worked
days at Plymouth—the music
I lived for, created by men
becoming myths. Twenty-five years
would pass before Brownie's pure voice
would find me again, on the road
this time, heading south to Fresno,
the FM station fading in
and out on the car's radio,
that sound never to be forgotten,
a gift I did nothing to earn.
Twenty-five years and nothing changed
for me; I made it home, I sat
alone and silent. The open

window gave me a dark wind
freighted with late September
and the smell of burning fuel
stinging my eyes unless I
was crying for the joy of being
whole in a country at war.
I had eaten and would eat
once more when I wakened long
after dawn: eggs I scrambled, toast
I buttered, potatoes, coffee
without cream. All that bright morning
I was free and owned myself.

THE THREE CROWS

At dawn my great aunt Tsipie would rise and go
to the east windows of the apartment,
face the weak October sun and curse God.
A deeply spiritual woman, she could roll
strudel dough so fine even the blind could see through it.
Overweight, 62, worn out
from mothering three daughters and one husband
—an upholsterer on nights at Dodge Main—
she no longer walked on water or raised
the recently dead. Instead she convened
at noon from her seventh story back porch
with heaven's emissaries, three black crows
perched in the top branches of the neighborhood's
one remaining oak. Stuffed with strudel,
safely inside the screen door, I heard
her speak out in Ukranian Yiddish
addressing the three angels by their names.
They would flutter their greasy, savage wings
in warning and settle back. "Fuck with me,"
they seemed to say, "You fuck with Him on high."
The hardness of eyes, the sureness of claws,
the incessant caw-cawing of their voices,
the incandescence of feathered wings,
of gleaming beaks, all this she faced down.
Who brought the sharp wheeze to her grandson's chest?
Who left her youngest simple? Who put Jake,
her husband, crooked back and all, on nights?
For minutes on end the three crows listened
and gave nothing in return. I could say
to all those who live in God's green kingdom,
her grandson grew into a tall young man,
Jake made it to days, simple Annie,
her daughter, learned to sew by hand at last,
for in truth all this happened. Even Yenkel,
her dearest brother, given up for lost
thirty years before, escaped from prison
in the pine forest of Siberia

to make his way to Michigan. Can you hear
the ax buried in a foreign tree, the child
floating like ashes above the lost town,
can you hear the vanished world? I remember
the three crows, especially their silences.
I remember Tsipie's voice, high and sweet,
going out on her breath of milk and tea,
asking to be heard. When the crows took off,
I remember the high branches quivering
before the world stilled. The three birds rose
imperiously above the roof tops
until they disappeared into a sky
long ago gone gray above our lives,
only to plummet surely back to earth.

PHOTOGRAPHY 2

Across the road from Ford's a Mrs. Strempek
planted tulip bulbs and irises even though
the remnants of winter were still hanging on
in gray speckled mounds. Smoking at all times
she would kneel, bare legged, on the hard ground
and half smile when I passed coming or going
as she worked her trowel back and forth for hours
making a little stubborn hole and when that
was done making another.
　　　　　　　　　　When Charles Sheeler
came to Dearborn to take his famous photographs
of the great Rouge plant he caught some workers,
tiny little men, at a distance, dwarfed
under the weight of the tools they thought
they commanded. When they got too close
he left them out of focus, gray lumps with white
wild eyes. Mainly he was interested in
the way space got divided or how light
changed nothing.
　　　　　　　　　　Nowhere does Mrs. Strempek
show up in all the records of that year,
nor do the few pale tulips and irises
that bloomed in the yard of her rented house
long gone to fire. For the first time I was
in love that spring and would walk the long mile
from the bus stop knowing it was useless,
at my feet the rutted tracks the trucks made,
still half frozen. Ahead the slag heaps
burning at all hours, and the great stacks
blackening the sky, and nothing in between.

REINVENTING AMERICA

The city was huge. A boy of twelve could walk
for hours while the closed houses stared down at him
from early morning to dusk, and he'd get nowhere.
Oh no, I was not that boy. Even at twelve I knew
enough to stay in my own neighborhood,
I knew anyone who left might not return.
Boys were animals with animal hungers
I learned early. Better to stay close to home.
I'd try to bum cigarettes from the night workers
as they left the bars in the heavy light of noon
or I'd hang around the grocery hoping
one of the beautiful young wives would ask me
to help her carry her shopping bags home.
You're wondering what I was up to. Not much.
The sun rose late in November and set early.
At times I thought life was rushing by too fast.
Before I knew it I'd be my half-blind uncle
married to a woman who cried all day long
while in the basement he passed his time working
on short-wave radio calls to anywhere.
I'd sneak down and talk to him, Uncle Nathan,
wiry in his boxer's shorts and high-topped boots,
chewing on a cigar, the one dead eye catching
the overhead light while he mused on his life
on the road or at sea. How he loved the whores
in the little Western towns or the Latin ports!
He'd hold his hands out to approximate
their perfect breasts. The months in jail had taught him
a man had only his honor and his ass
to protect. "You turn your fist this way," he said,
taking my small hand in both of his, "and fire
from the shoulder, so," and he'd extend it out
to the face of an imaginary foe.
Why he'd returned to this I never figured out,
though life was ample here, a grid of crowded blocks
of Germans, Wops, Polacks, Jews, wild Irish,
plus some square heads from the Upper Peninsula.

Six bakeries, four barber shops, a five and dime,
twenty beer gardens, a Catholic church with a *shul*
next door where we studied the Talmud-Torah.
Wonderful how all the old hatreds bubbled
so quietly on the back burner you could
forget until one day they tore through the pool halls,
the bowling alley, the high school athletic fields
leaving an eye gone, a long fresh, livid scar
running to touch a mouth, young hands raw or broken,
boys and girls ashamed of what they were, ashamed
of what they were not. It was merely village life,
exactly what our parents left in Europe
brought to America with pure fidelity.

THE CAFE

Everything goes on in the cafe behind the rail yard.
The two women who work the bar are from Albania,
so the men try not to look down their blouses
for fear of their brother, Anton, who sits alone
smoking and slowly drinking the pink wine of Michigan.

Have you ever had the pink wine of Michigan? They say
it's made from watermelons and rancid strawberries,
that it smells like old socks, that too much drives you nuts.
When Anton has too much he likes to sing songs of home
to the workers at the bar who understand nothing.

The women flirt shamelessly. They run their tongues
over their teeth, they roll their eyes heavenward,
they bend over every chance they get so their skirts
ride up the backs of their thighs. Anton goes out into
the night to piss on the truck tires and curse God.

Even Jerome, our weightlifter, won't cross Anton
though he bullies the rest of us. "Schemansky and the Jew
beat me out," he says, "a Polack and a kike."
We'll hear the story a thousand years, how he went
two days by Greyhound to the trials just to lose,

how he was cheated, how he was the real winner.
He spits all this into my face, the shame of his loss
flooding his scalp with blood, the small pale eyes
frozen in their sockets. He never even saw New Orleans.
Took the first bus home and hid in his room for days.

From the rail yard you can hear the boxcars coupling
and uncoupling, the switch engines starting up or braking.
Even after it rains you can look up and not see
the moon or stars. I stood one night for twenty minutes
staring up until my eyes tired and it began to rain.

Louisa, the younger girl, has blue-black hair
she leaves unbound and deep brown eyes. If you stare
into those eyes she will stare back, if you reach
across the bar to place a hand on the damp hand
she rests on the bar she won't withdraw hers.

The night Bernard said he loved her she smiled,
unclenched her teeth, and said, "Now you must marry me."
Anton said he was phoning a priest that second
so he could give her away. Bernard sobered up
with coffee, a bowl of soup, and two hard-boiled eggs.

No one ever saw Bernard again. They say Anton cut him.
I don't think so. Some nights the workers just drink
in silence, the air thickens with smoke, and no one cares
if the two girls show their thighs or their breasts, some nights
the young men along the bar are too tired even to die.

SALT AND OIL

Three young men in dirty work clothes
on their way home or to a bar
in the late morning. This is not
a photograph, it is a moment
in the daily life of the world,
a moment that will pass into
the unwritten biography
of your city or my city
unless it is frozen in the fine print
of our eyes. I turn away
to read the morning paper and lose
the words. I go into the streets
for an hour or more, walking slowly
for even a man of my age. I buy
an apple but do not eat it.
The old woman who sells it remarks
on its texture and tartness, she
laughs and the veins of her cheeks brown.
I stare into the river while time
refuses to move. Meanwhile the three
begin to fade, giving up
their names and voices, their auras
of smoke and grease, their acrid bouquets.
We shall name one to preserve him,
we shall name him *Salt*, the tall blond
whose wrists hurt, who is holding back
something, curses or tears, and shaking
out the exhaustion, his blue eyes
swollen with sleeplessness, his words
blasted on the horn of his breath.
We could go into the cathedral
of his boyhood and recapture
the voices that were his, we could
reclaim him from the brink of fire,
but then we would lose the other,
the one we call *Oil*, for Oil
broods in the tiny crevices

between then and now, Oil survives
in the locked archives of the clock.
His one letter proclaims, "My Dear
President, I would rather not . . ."
One arm draped across the back
of Salt, his mouth wide with laughter,
the black hair blurring the forehead,
he extends his right hand, open
and filthy to take rusted chains,
frozen bearings, the scarred hands
of strangers, there is nothing
he will not take. These two are not
brothers, the one tall and solemn,
the long Slavic nose, the pale eyes,
the puffed mouth offended by the press
of traffic, while the twin is glad
to be with us on this late morning
in paradise. If you asked him,
"Do you calm the roiling waters?"
he would smile and shake his great head,
unsure of your meaning. If you asked
the sources of his glee he would shrug
his thick shoulders and roll his eyes
upward to where the turning leaves
take the wind, and the gray city birds
dart toward their prey, and flat clouds
pencil their obscure testaments
on the air. For a moment
the energy that makes them who
they are shatters the noon's light
into our eyes, and when we see
again they are gone and the street
is quiet, the day passing into
evening, and this is autumn
in the present year. "The third man,"
you ask, "who was the third man
in the photograph?" There is no

photograph, no mystery,
only Salt and Oil
in the daily round of the world,
three young men in dirty work clothes
on their way under a halo
of torn clouds and famished city birds.
There is smoke and grease, there is
the wrist's exhaustion, there is laughter,
there is the letter seized in the clock
and the apple's tang, the river
sliding along its banks, darker
now than the sky descending
a last time to scatter its diamonds
into these black waters that contain
the day that passed, the night to come.

II

JOE GOULD'S PEN

I am told this is the pen,
that it will write for me too
if I let it have its way,
that it will be eloquent
as only genius can be,
glad, bittersweet, profound, "blue,"
as we used to say when we
indulged ourselves, also to
the point, precise in detail
when sketching the actual,
but able always to dash
off into the unreal at
any moment. Poised over
the paper, I wait, then write:
"Later when the candle died
she could see the day begin
between the ash cans and the larch,
so she rose." Is her hair blond,
black, gray? Does she bow her head
when I reach to stroke her and
rise slowly against my palm
as a cat might? The pen asks
much more than it can answer,
one word at a time. "The Owl,
the Alabama, the Grand,
Newport, Crystal, White House,
the Progress, the Marathon,
the Lion, all on the Bowery
in nineteen and forty-one,
each one fifty cents a night,
each one once my home sweet home."
Even the cheap post office ink
knows the universe does not
exist anymore. Slugs closed,
no more cups of coffee for
nothing, no more samovars
steaming by the open door,

no more black gypsy goulash
on the back burner, no more
all-night Judgment Day sermons,
no more anything no more.
"Before dusk the sparrows came
back to pick at what crumbs of
rye bread toast the pigeons left
that morning." I'm following
the oral history of our times
as it forms itself letter
by letter on this blank school
book, but nowhere does it say
up or down, right or not right,
exit slowly, men at work,
smoking allowed, enter at
your own risk, two for the price
of one, nowhere does it say
house for sale, this land is mine,
attack cat on premises.
"If we had time I could take
you to García Lorca's
unknown graveyard, the run-down
old Jewish one off St. James.
We could lean against the stones,
converse, and eat egg salad
sandwiches. The dead would not
mind; in fact the dead are gone.
They were so gaunt they slipped
through the rusting gate one night
and walked to Jerusalem."
Joe Gould's pen wrote those ten lines
hoping to capture his sense
of the ridiculousness
of the life he was born to,
to hint at the wealth that came
so close to him he could taste
it all the rest of his life

smeared with ketchup. Pee Wee Joe,
who loved to dance, who talked
to seagulls in their language,
his pen tried to find him in
9,250,000
words and failed because it had
no word for what rises in
your esophagus when night
starts over at 4 A.M.,
no word for the itch you can't
scratch, no word for the bubble
of pain that rises slowly
to settle underneath your heart.
We could say "heartburn," but that
doesn't begin to do it,
we could say "anxiety,"
"terror," "loneliness," "despair,"
and still not get anywhere
closer than he did with his
9,250,000
words that vanished into blue
hospital air before he
turned to the wall and welcomed
the last act. He had a word
for that—we all do—but no
word for a woman's shoulders
as she rises from her bed
in the darkness, no word even
for the warm darkness smelling
of one ocean and the seven
rivers that surround the heart,
no word for the wind flattening
the motherwort that grows at
its ease in the public squares
or along the cracked curbing
on Delancey Street, the wind
bringing hope in the morning

and carrying off our exhaust
as the light goes each evening.
Don't blame the pen with its chromed
steel nib and fat black plastic
body that for forty years
contained the dark lexicon
of the mystery of one
little man and missed the point.
"You'd find him in the downtown
libraries," someone wrote, "at
all hours filling page after
page, scribbling furiously,
always chasing the last word."
He carried his swollen books
in a cardboard folder stained
with black coffee and clutched
to his chest as though they were
his own life. Perhaps they were.
Perhaps he knew that when
he gave back the last hard breath
each earned word would disappear
the way the golden halo
goes when the dawn shreds the rose
into dust, the way a voice fades
in an empty room, the way
the pomegranate fallen from
the tree scatters the seeds of
its resurrection, the way
these lines are vanishing now.

THE SEARCH FOR LORCA'S SHADOW

I've seen the hillside. A soft wind moved
through the leaves of the olive trees. Yes,
this is a poem about historic death,
it would be incomplete without hillsides
thick with olive trees, their leaves turning
silver as the land wind shivers them.
The earth, by which I mean the soil, the dirt,
is a metallic gray covered here and there
by a loamy dust which may or may not
shift in the breeze. The ants come and go
doing their dull work. They are alive,
they are going about the business
of their lives, building their dwellings,
providing, eating as best they can.
They do not remember the victim.
They did not even know his name, his voice
which rings still in the voices of others,
his dark hair fallen across one eye,
his rages and jealousies, his body
clothed in worn cotton garments sewn by hand.
(Were he alive he could look carefully
at the bloodstained shirt, count the stitches
that attached the cuffs, and tell you, "No,
that is not the work of my grandmother.")
Forgive the ants, they are merely ants,
though they are alive and he is not,
though they would surely eat him if they could,
if in fact anything were left to eat—
the bones are here as clean as porcelain,
for the earth has long ago eaten all
there was to eat. First forgive the ants
or we'll get nowhere in this useless search
for the darkness he was and the darkness
he became. It is August. The noon sun
pours down on this merciless landscape
that watched with its thousand eyes hidden
in the gashed trunks and the undersides

of gray stones and did nothing. Someone
wrote, "The crime was in Granada,"
though actually it was here among ants,
stones, dust, olive trees, fallen fruit, the boots
of armed men, the cries of women and men
where now there is only silence and no
darkness we can say is his, Federico's.

THE SEA WE READ ABOUT

Now and then a lost sea gull flutters into
our valley, comes down in a burned cotton field
and simply gives up. Once I left my pickup
by the side of the road, dug a square grave
the size of a beer case, and dropped in the bird.
Quintero, the short, husky truck farmer
from Tranquility, stopped to call out. What was I
doing in late July under the noon sun
digging in someone else's field? I told him.
Slowly he unwound himself from the truck's cab,
took up his shovel, and trudged over to see
it was done right. After we tamped down the earth
we stood speechless in the middle of nothing
while a hot wind whispered through the miles of stalks
and Johnson grass. "Can you hear what it's saying?"
Quintero asked. For the first time I noticed his eyes
were green and one didn't move. "Been hearing it
all my life, 62 years," and head down under
the straw cowboy hat he turned to go, waving
a thick forearm at the sky. I should have asked.
I'd seen him often before, stooped in his field of melons,
pensive, still, and took him for part of the place,
one more doomed farmer. An hour later, nursing
a cold beer, I stood outside the 7-11
at the four corners listening, but the voices
inside kept breaking in, two young drivers
teasing the pregnant girl who worked the register,
her laughter egging them on. Suddenly the bearded,
shirtless one began to sing a Beatles' song,
"Why Don't We Do It in the Road," in such a pure voice
my whole world froze. Twenty-four years ago,
the war was ending, and though I wasn't young
I believed the land rose westward toward mountains
hidden in dust and smog and beyond the mountains
the sea spread out, limitless and changing
everything, and that I would get there some day.

SUNDAYS WITH LUNGO

Lungo and I would go into the deep woods
on Sunday mornings before the town woke.
I think he was looking for something rare,
a sign maybe, a stream carved from gray snow,
wild wisteria that grows like weeds down here,
or perhaps a pale crocus or robin eggs.
You couldn't tell with Lungo, he said so little,
and what he said came sideways out of his mouth
so the wind would blow it to tatters, words
that became nothing. He'd stop abruptly,
drop to one knee, move a few twigs and leaves,
then rise and go on. It was his mission,
I liked to think, and I was simply there
as the witness to his perseverance.
We'd go on until we broke into light
at the river's edge. On the other side
more dark woods stood as a silent rebuke
to Lungo's quest, if quest it was. He'd shake
his great white head, and the laughter would burst
like song from his thin chest, for we were stopped.
No, we weren't boys. We were men, not young men
either though young men do useless things
year after year for the sake of doing.
Before he died I knew what was coming
because in those last weeks I heard his voice
suddenly surging and roaring, not words,
or at least not words I knew, just pure sounds
thrust back into the wind's face, and his face—
already deeply carved—darkened with joy.
That last Sunday when we found the river
rain was falling softly into the leaves
behind us, and the gray waters swept by
hiding their mysteries and the far woods
glistened with promise. "This is it," he said,
and dropped to both knees and closed his eyes up
so tightly not a single tear escaped.
I came back once, alone, looking for him,

for all he spoke or beckoned to, and found
something familiar. I stopped long before
I reached the river; the wind was speaking
in the top branches of the sycamores
telling me he was here if anywhere.
Do you know how to read the wind? Do you?
It's easy. Just close your eyes and listen.
Of course you have to be old, broken
in body and spirit, brought down so low—
as Lungo was—that even words make sense.

THE UNKNOWABLE

Practicing his horn on the Williamsburg Bridge
hour after hour, "woodshedding" the musicians
called it, but his woodshed was the world.

The enormous tone he borrowed from Hawkins
that could fill a club to overflowing
blown into tatters by the sea winds

teaching him humility, which he carries
with him at all times, not as an amulet
against the powers of animals and men

that mean harm or the lure of the marketplace.
No, a quality of the gaze downward
on the streets of Brooklyn or Manhattan.

Hold his hand and you'll see it, hold his eyes
in yours and you'll hear the wind singing
through the cables of the bridge that was home,

singing through his breath—no rarer than yours,
though his became the music of the world
thirty years ago. Today I ask myself

how he knew the time had come to inhabit
the voice of the air and how later
he decided the time had come for silence,

for the world to speak any way it could?
He wouldn't answer because he'd find
the question pompous. He plays for money.

The years pass, and like the rest of us
he ages, his hair and beard whiten, the great
shoulders narrow. He is merely a man—

after all—a man who stared for years
into the breathy, unknowable voice
of silence and captured the music.

I CAUGHT A GLIMPSE

It happens when I've been driving
   for hours on two-lane roads winding
      past orchards just after they've bloomed.

When I ask myself where I was when all
   this burst like the bounty of heaven, no
      answer comes back from the earth or heaven.

A hint of rain is in the air and the sky
   broods above a sudden stand of oak that
      rushes by. Between the trees coming

into the new green of their leaves light
   breaks for a second and within the light a path
      opens through the trees and the fields beyond.

Beyond, unseen, an ancient river runs
   high in its banks bringing the Sierras' gift
      back down to earth. The moment is so full

I have to close my eyes and slow the car.
   Should I go back the long, abandoned roads
      that lead me to this place and this moment

to find why I've become who I am
   and why that could matter. Slowly now
      I pass through a small town of scrubbed houses,

wide lawns, and empty streets. A rain has passed
   leaving little pools reflecting the sky
      that stares open-eyed at its own image.

If this were Sunday the bells would ring,
   if this were sixty years ago I
      would be a boy on foot no farther

than I am now with my eyes filled
    with so much seeing. I caught a glimpse,
        a road through the trees, a door

that opened a moment only to close.
    Twelve miles from Stockton. I could go west
        until I reached the sea or keep going

farther and farther into this valley
    past the truck stops and the ruined towns
        while the afternoon closes down around me.

NIGHT WORDS

after Juan Ramon

A child wakens in a cold apartment.
The windows are frosted. Outside he hears
words rising from the streets, words he cannot
understand, and then the semis gear down
for the traffic light on Houston. He sleeps
again and dreams of another city
on a high hill above a wide river
bathed in sunlight, and the dream is his life
as he will live it twenty years from now.
No, no, you say, dreams do not work that way,
they function otherwise. Perhaps in the world
you're right, but on Houston tonight two men
are trying to change a tire as snow gathers
on their shoulders and scalds their ungloved hands.
The older one, the father, is close to tears,
for he's sure his son, who's drunk, is laughing
secretly at him for all his failures
as a man and a father, and he is
laughing to himself but because he's happy
to be alone with his father as he was
years ago in another life where snow
never fell. At last he slips the tire iron
gently from his father's grip and kneels down
in the unstained snow and unbolts the wheel
while he sings of drinking a glass of wine,
the black common wine of Alicante,
in raw sunlight. Now the father joins in,
and the words rise between the falling flakes
only to be transformed into the music
spreading slowly over the oiled surface
of the river that runs through every child's dreams.

ONCE

Hungry and cold, I stood in a doorway
on Delancey Street in 1946
as the rain came down. The worst part is this
is not from a bad movie. I'd read Dos Passos
USA and thought, "Before the night ends
my life will change." A stranger would stop
to ask for my help, a single stranger
more needy than I, if such a woman
were possible. I still had cigarettes,
damp matches, and an inaccurate map
of Manhattan in my head, and the change
from the one $20 Travelers Check
I'd cashed in a dairy restaurant where
the amazed owner actually proclaimed
to the busy heads, "They got Jews in Detroit!"

You can forgive the night. No one else was dumb
enough to be out. Sure, it was Easter.
Was I expecting crocus and lilac
to burst from the pavement and sweeten
the air the way they did in Michigan once
upon a time? This wouldn't be so bad
if you were only young once. Once would be fine.
You stand out in the rain once and get wet
expecting to enter fiction. You huddle
under the Williamsburg Bridge posing for *Life*.
You trek to the Owl Hotel to lie awake
in a room the size of a cat box and smell
the dawn as it leaks under the shade
with the damp welcome you deserve. Just the once
you earn your doctorate in mismanagement.

So I was eighteen, once, fifty years ago,
a kid from a small town with big ideas.
Gatsby said if Detroit is your idea
of a small town you need another idea,
and I needed several. I retied my shoes, washed

my face, brushed my teeth with a furry tongue,
counted out my $11.80
on the broken bed, and decided the time
had come to mature. How else can I explain
voting for Adlai Stevenson once and once
again, planting a lemon tree in hard pan,
loaning my Charlie Parker 78s
to an out-of-work actor, eating pork loin
barbecued on Passover, tangoing
perfectly without music even with you?

PHILOSOPHY LESSON

After driving all night long
I stopped for coffee and eggs
at a diner halfway to
New York City. The waitress
behind the counter looked up
from her magazine and said,
"Look who's here!" clapped her hands
together and broke into
a huge smile. "Have I been here
before?" I asked. "Beats the shit
out of me," she said and put
a glass of cloudy water
in front of me. "What'll it be?"
One war was closing down
in Asia to be followed
by another. No longer
a kid, I wondered who was
I that a gray-haired woman
up all night in a road-side
hole would greet me like a star.
"What do you think of Sartre
and the Existentialists?"
I asked. "We get the eggs fresh
from down the road, my old man
bakes the bread and sweet rolls.
It's all good." It's not often
you get the perfect answer
to such a profound question.
On the way back to the truck
I listened to the pebbles
crunching under my wing-tips,
watched two huge crows watching me
from a sad maple, smelled
the fishy air blowing in
from Lake Erie, and thought, "Some
things are too good to be true."

"HE WOULD NEVER USE ONE WORD
WHERE NONE WOULD DO"

If you said, "Nice day," he would look up
at the three clouds riding overhead,
nod at each, and go back to doing what-
ever he was doing or not doing.
If you asked for a smoke or a light,
he'd hand you whatever he found
in his pockets: a jackknife, a hankie—
usually unsoiled—a dollar bill,
a subway token. Once he gave me
half the sandwich he was eating
at the little outdoor restaurant
on Laguardia Place. I remember
a single sparrow was perched on the back
of his chair, and when he held out
a piece of bread on his open palm,
the bird snatched it up and went back to
its place without even a thank you,
one hard eye staring at my bad eye
as though I were next. That was in May
of '97, spring had come late,
but the sun warmed both of us for hours
while silence prevailed, if you can call
the blaring of taxi horns and the trucks
fighting for parking and the kids on skates
streaming past silence. My friend Frankie
was such a comfort to me that year,
the year of the crisis. He would turn
up his great dark head just going gray
until his eyes met mine, and that was all
I needed to go on talking nonsense
as he sat patiently waiting me out,
the bird staring over his shoulder.
"Silence is silver," my Zaydee had said,
getting it wrong and right, just as he said,

"Water is thicker than blood," thinking
this made him a real American.
Frankie was already American
being half German, half Indian.
Fact is silence is the perfect water:
unlike rain it falls from no clouds
to wash our minds, to ease our tired eyes,
to give heart to the thin blades of grass
fighting through the concrete for even air
dirtied by our endless stream of words.

THE MORTAL WORDS OF ZWEIK

As an old man, Zweik told me
he was afraid of aspirin,
one tablet and he didn't
know who he was. He is gone
sixteen years now and no one
reads his novels anymore.
A few recall a squat fellow
bicycling to the market
on cold mornings for the coffee
and howling at the clerks when
there was no sugar or cream.
When I was in 6th grade he
was only a name to me
until Dougie Harris sent
him a personal letter
as part of a book report
assignment. Three weeks later
a long, hand-written answer
came back that explained he wrote
because there was nothing else
he could do well. It was work,
but you got to set your hours
and though the pay wasn't great
he had hopes. A movie was
being made of his last book
so maybe . . . "Stay warm and dry
in Detroit, and give my best
to your teacher, Miss Hardman."
The class was stunned. A great man
had written Dougie Harris,
the unfolded pages lay
upon his desk curling in
the winter light, and we sat
in silence for a minute
as though life would never be
the same. Miss Hardman spoke first;
I can no longer recall

what she said or if she said
anything or just returned
us to an ordinary
afternoon in Michigan
in time for the bell to ring.
Dougie Harris died before
he was thirty-five, leaving
a wife and kids. The letter
passed from hand to hand, unread,
then into a bundle tied
with string that frayed and later
broke so that the pages fell
of their own accord onto
a cellar floor and were swept up
by someone who meant no harm
only to be transformed into
fire, smoke, then nothing. The words
kept their silence for a time
and then joined with other words
to form sentences scattered
across the backs of postcards.
Translated into French they
now make up the final verse
of an anthem condemning
Catholics, while the last one
slips slowly from its shred of truth
syllable by syllable.
Miss Hardman later married
and so was scalded by that
particular disappointment.
Waking in a hospital ward
west of Bratislava, Zweik
had no idea who he was
and no time to find out.
These days those classmates read
brochures for retirement homes
in Lompoc or the Smokies

but not one notices the same
light has entered their studies
as though kept in a black box
for sixty years, not the light
of history or great painting
or theater, just the late light
of January afternoons
that answers everything.

LITTLE APPLE OF MY EYE

Varenna, Italy
In the park leading to the post office
each morning on the way to collect the mail I don't get
I meet the same woman coming slowly up
the steep stairway that leads to the upper town.

Short, thick hipped, bundled up in sweaters,
scarves, a thick wool coat, she is led by
a small black and white dog straining first
one way and then another against the leash.

There is such patience and tenderness for the dog
that for some weeks I took her to be an English woman,
so many endearments repeated over and over,
one of which I heard as, "Little apple of my eye."

*

Late October chill. At dawn the lake dreams
in the heavy mist. The tall cypresses stand out
against the far hillsides going yellow and red.
By ten the rain is settling on the wet leaves

of the maples and chestnuts below my window.
In jacket, raincoat, boots, and hat I start down
the trail that leads to town. The woman is not English.
Her husband was the wild butcher who founded

the town's antique motorcycle club after the war,
before he ran off the road to Lecco and broke his hip,
before he was stapled back together and left her
for good on his BMW stolen from the Afrika Korps.

*

*

The woman is not English. She did not say,
"Little apple of my eye." God knows what she said.
Today she comes toward me, her hair plastered down
under a red silk scarf, chanting her endearments

to little Foxly, his coat as wet as hers, his nails
skidding on the bricks of the stairs, pulling one way,
then another as she stumbles behind him cooing,
"Little apple of my eye," as the rain streams down.

Everyone has a story. If you linger long enough
outside the post office or in the tobacco shop,
they'll tell you the day the mad butcher returned
seven years later with a white beard and a new woman.

*

In the Protestant cemetery rests the old gentleman
who came to town to drink the white waters
of the Fiumelatte, the river of milk, he thought
would cure his migraines. Daily he trooped up and down

these hills with Foxly behind, in rain and sunshine,
hoping also to clear his poor lungs of Nottingham.
Somehow he never noticed the poisonous clouds drifting
over the south end of the lake, a gift from Milan

that stained the windows of his rooms a greasy yellow.
When he stood, apoplectic, in the post office, stamping
his cane and demanding attention, the dog at his side,
he did not shout out, "Little apple of my eye."

*

*

The tan 1939 BMW 500 c.c., now with side car
for the young wife and genuine gas mask canister,
sulks all afternoon in the rain outside the butcher shop.
They say he cuts the best veal in town, thin as paper,

sells to the best hotels and the villas up on the hills.
When with his good leg he fires up the motorcycle
the whole town can hear it. Everyone knows everything
about these lives, their comings and goings.

They do not know who said, "Little apple of my eye."
Even I, the only one who heard it, will never know.
Tomorrow a clear, cold day will break over the lake
pouring its soft light down on all the secret houses.

III

CLOUDS ABOVE THE SEA

My father and mother, two tiny figures,
side by side, facing the clouds that move
in from the Atlantic. August, '33.
The whole weight of the rain to come, the weight
of all that has fallen on their houses
gathers for a last onslaught, and yet they
hold, side by side, in the eye of memory.
What was she wearing, you ask, what did he
say to make the riding clouds hold their breath?
Our late August afternoons were chilly
in America, so I shall drape her throat
in a silken scarf above a black dress.

I could give her a rope of genuine pearls
as a gift for bearing my father's sons,
and let each pearl glow with a child's fire.
I could turn her toward you now with a smile
so that we might joy in her constancy,
I could bury the past in dust rising,
dense rain falling, and the absence of sky
so that you could turn this page and smile.
My father and mother, two tiny figures,
side by side, facing the clouds that move
in from the Atlantic. They are silent
under the whole weight of the rain to come.

THE NEW WORLD

A man roams the streets with a basket
of freestone peaches hollering, "Peaches,
peaches, yellow freestone peaches for sale."

My grandfather in his prime could outshout
the Tigers of Wrath or the factory whistles
along the river. Hamtramck hungered

for yellow freestone peaches, downriver
wakened from a dream of work, Zug Island danced
into the bright day glad to be alive.

Full-figured women in their negligees
streamed into the streets from the dark doorways
to demand in Polish or Armenian

the ripened offerings of this new world.
Josepf Prisckulnick out of Dubrovica
to Detroit by way of Ellis Island

raised himself regally to his full height
of five feet two and transacted until
the fruit was gone into those eager hands.

Thus would there be a letter sent across
an ocean and a continent and thus
would Sadie waken to the news of wealth

without limit in the bright and distant land
and thus bags were packed and she set sail
for America. Some of this is true.

The women were gaunt. All day the kids dug
in the back lots searching for anything.
The place was Russia with another name.

Joe was five feet two. Dubrovica burned
to gray ashes the west wind carried off,
then Rovno went, then the Dneiper turned to dust.

We sat around the table telling lies
while the late light filled an empty glass.
Bread, onions, the smell of burning butter,

small white potatoes we shared with no one
because the hour was wrong, the guest was late,
and this was Michigan in 1928.

AFTER THE WAR

for Ingo Richter

Six little clusters of houses
in a valley and between them
meadows, tilled fields, orchards
of apple trees where the bees
roam on summer evenings.
A father, a mother, and son
walk together in silence
the long miles in the late light.
It is Saturday, and they
are going to dinner on Saturday.
When they arrive the men clasp
hands out in the yard, the boy
removes his cap, the door opens
so they can enter. The door
closes so the late light
is kept out. From the far end
of the valley a great noise
rolls in through the orchards
to stop against the bright house.
At table the boy hears and bows
his head. The others go on talking.
Three years now the terrible war
is over, so it must be
the voice of a fire raging
among the apple trees or the oxen
moaning over their fate or
no noise at all, merely blood
pounding in the boy's temples.
I would say it is blood pounding
in the boy's temples if I too
had not heard the fire raging
and the oxen moaning and all
the bees screaming as the light
went out in the apple orchards.
The father, the mother, the son
must walk the dark miles back
on the narrow dirt road not

whitened by moonlight. The three
walk in single file with father
taking the lead. There are stars
above, for it is September
when no rain falls. There are stars
too in the winter, distant, cold.
There are distant stars always
staring down with the bright eyes
of owls or the damp, wise eyes
of grandparents guiding the three
down the dark road toward their silence.

BLACK STONE ON TOP OF NOTHING

Still sober, César Vallejo comes home and finds a black ribbon
around the apartment building covering the front door.
He puts down his cane, removes his greasy fedora, and begins
to untangle the mess. His neighbors line up behind him
wondering what's going on. A middle-aged woman carrying
a loaf of fresh bread asks him to step aside so she
can enter, ascend the two steep flights to her apartment,
and begin the daily task of preparing lunch for her Monsieur.
Vallejo pretends he hears nothing or perhaps he truly
hears nothing so absorbed is he in this odd task consuming
his late morning. Did I forget to mention that no one else
can see the black ribbon or understand why his fingers
seem so intent on unraveling what is not there? Remember
when you were only six and on especially hot days you
would descend the shaky steps to the cellar hoping at first
that someone, perhaps your mother, would gradually
become aware of your absence and feel a sudden seizure
of anxiety or terror. Of course no one noticed. Mother
sat for hours beside the phone waiting, and now and then
gazed at summer sunlight blazing through the parlor curtains
while below, cool and alone, seated on the damp concrete
you watched the same sunlight filter through the rising dust
from the two high windows. Beside the furnace a spider
worked brilliantly downward from the burned-out, overhead bulb
with a purpose you at that age could still comprehend.
1937 would last only six more months. It was a Thursday.
Rain was promised but never arrived. The brown spider worked
with or without hope, though when the dusty sunlight caught
in the web you beheld a design so perfect it remained
in your memory as a model of meaning. César Vallejo
untangled the black ribbon no one else saw and climbed
to his attic apartment and gazed out at the sullen rooftops
stretching southward toward Spain where his heart died. I know this.
I've walked by the same building year after year in late evening
when the swallows were settling noiselessly in the few sparse trees
beside the unused canal. I've come when the winter snow
blinded the distant brooding sky. I've come just after dawn,
I've come in spring, in autumn, in rain, and he was never there.

THE DEAD

A good man is seized by the police
and spirited away. Months later
someone brags that he shot him once
through the back of the head
with a Walther P 38, and his life
ended just there. Those who loved
him go on searching the cafes
in the Barrio Chino or the bars
near the harbor. A comrade swears
he saw him at a distance buying
two kilos of oranges in the market
of San José and called out, "Andrés,
Andrés," but instead of turning
to a man he'd known since child-
hood and opening his great arms
wide, he scurried off, the oranges
tumbling out of the damp sack, one
after another, a short bright trail
left on the sidewalk to say,
Farewell! Farewell to what? I ask.
I asked then and I ask now. I first
heard the story fifty years ago;
it became part of the mythology I
hauled with me from one graveyard
to another, this belief in the power
of my yearning. The dead are every-
where, crowding the narrow streets
that jut out from the wide boulevard
on which we take our morning walk.
They stand in the cold shadows
of men and women come to sell
themselves to anyone, they stride
along beside me and stop when I
stop to admire the bright garlands
or the little pyramids of fruit,
they reach a hand out to give
money or to take change, they say

"Good morning" or "Thank you," they
turn with me and retrace my steps
back to the bare little room I've
come to call home. Patiently,
they stand beside me staring out
over the soiled roofs of the world
until the light fades and we are
all one or no one. They ask for
so little, a prayer now and then,
a toast to their health which is
our health, a few lies no one reads
incised on a dull plaque between
a pharmacy and a sports store,
the least little daily miracle.

THE EVENING TURNED ITS BACK
UPON HER VOICE

Is she waiting for a knock on the door
or a letter from someone she has never met?
The rain and the night are coming down as one
as she knew they would. Forty years ago,

a gray hotel across from the terminal.
She sits in the wooden chair, my sister,
her hands crossed in her lap, her eyes cast down,
no longer listening for a voice, yours or mine,

carried on wet winds across the broken years.
Tomorrow it will be 1956
for the first time. The shadows do not know
this, nor does the bare bulb swaying above,

nor does the swollen river with its name
of orange blossoms and silt, nor does the moon
no one sings to. You and I, sitting side
by side, leafing through the great book of days

know it now. You trace a forefinger down
the crowded page and find her name, misspelled
but here, the three curious, foreign names,
her only life crowded into the slack letters

that say nothing of her hands, pale and strong,
the black nails broken by work, or of her voice,
of how it hung like smoke in that bare room,
of how it calls and calls to us without words.

THESE WORDS

In the rainy cold weather of April
the wind deposits scraps of odd letters,
damp ragged stories only partly told
and left this morning outside my back door.
I, who believe in the beauty of words,
dry them in the oven until the paper
curls, and then I begin to decipher
their meaning if there is one or bestow
some meaning on them. On one page I find
my own name repeated over and over
by someone in need of help, a woman
wanting attention or love or money,
a woman I have never met writing
from Lexington. A spurt of rain blurred
some words, so simply printed, but I find
"manic depressive" and "beautiful" on
the same line. She is writing about some-
one else, a woman we both know out of
our separate pasts, a woman terribly
in need of my help. An institution
is named, one in Virginia, that admits
such cases. Will I act out of the love
we once had for each other? Will I act
now while there is time? "Phillip," she writes,
misspelling my name, "you are all that stands
between your cousin Pearl and hopelessness."
I go to the window. Iris and rose
shiver in the cold wind. My cousin Pearl
died three years ago, alone, in Bellevue,
refusing to see me. "I want you to
remember me as I was," her note said.
I know that you too receive such letters,
that these words find their way from door to door,
that the words themselves have meaning and are
dignified and beautiful as they march
across these grimy scraps of paper, that
they are all that stands between the darkness

the light suggests is not here and what is
here, words from someone we can never know
that have a meaning we can't comprehend.
"Door," she has written, "leaf," on the page's
other side, "stone," words out of poetry,
the words my mother read to Cousin Pearl
forty-nine years ago to comfort her
in her loss. How innocent we were then,
how much we believed in the comfort words
could bring, how much we thought they would explain,
though spring was late, the rain beat on the glass,
beat down on the mounded snow until the streets
ran with the clear ink of its meaning.

CESARE

One sorry town after another passed
the streaked windows of the train. We smoked, talked
of growing up, he near Torino,
I in Michigan. Born in a small town
in an inland valley, he loved the sea,
just walking along the shore, day or night,
filled with a joy he'd never known.
In my imagination even in the rain,
with his wool cap pulled down over one eye,
he passes the window of the cafe
like a ghost as the day fails. I see him
coming toward me now, tall, thin, myopic,
full of delight in his awkward body,
still only a boy with a boy's wide smile
as the rain streams down. You too must know
men like Cesare, still so young, brilliant,
full of plans and tall tales. Then women
enter their lives and the unfillable need
for tenderness. They fall in love, then
fall in love again and again and nothing
comes of it but heartbreak. And they are men,
so when you reach to touch them, to help them,
they turn away because men must do that.
Of course I never knew any Cesare,
he died before I left Detroit, before
I had a chance. I'm really talking
about someone else I can't name because
I simply can't, a man so singular
that when I lost him I had the train ride
I couldn't forget, Paris to somewhere
in early fall, the towns along the way
with their blackened churches, factories, shops,
cinemas all closed down. How did I miss
what was to come? It was all there in the rain.

When my uncle came home from Burma
he had a little blue scar beside
his right eye. "That was where the bullet
came out," he'd laugh, and when I asked
where it went in, he'd open his mouth,
point a long forefinger down his throat,
"Right there, we learned to eat everything."
Some days his given name was Nathan,
Nathan Hale, others Nathaniel Hawthorne.
No, he hadn't forgotten his name.
A grown man did not forget his name.
Under the grape arbor in August
uncle with his morning tea and milk,
a warm wind trembling the flat leaves.
He would stare up at the fruit hanging
in thick black clusters while slowly
sucking at his first unlit cigar.
"By eight the night was dark as that,
then it got darker." He'd flick the fruit
with the dry end and bare his stained teeth
in a huge smile without the least mirth.
The afternoons would grow so hot we'd
sleep for hours in a strange dream of sleep
to waken to the house chattering
in the evening breeze. I'd hear him
stumbling barefoot through the empty rooms
in search of something or someone he
would never name. The long days passed
into another season that brought
down the fruit in bunches. Bowed by rust
and their own great weight the sunflowers
came back to earth. At dusk the sky bled
in the west, blood shot through the dry leaves
of the alder and the oak, blood fell
from nowhere and puddled in the pale grass
until I thought the days would never end.
"It was autumn," uncle said, squatting

by the unlocked door to the tool shed.
"It was the beginning of autumn,
the little noiseless Asian rains poured
their waters down on us until we
slept on duty in our wet uniforms
leaning into each other like kittens.
A man alone would walk off the road
into an open field to find his sleep."
That afternoon he made a phone call
to someone I could tell he did not
know and chanted in a secret voice
that floated from room to room for hours.
Though no one came for uncle he dressed
in his one good suit, with the dark stripe,
his good white shirt starched and buttoned
at the throat. The little scar pulsed
beside the one blind eye filled with blood
while the other stared at nothing that
was there until the day's last light failed,
the room stilled, and we entered the past.

THE RETURN

All afternoon my father drove the country roads
between Detroit and Lansing. What he was looking for
I never learned, no doubt because he never knew himself,
though he would grab any unfamiliar side road
and follow where it led past fields of tall sweet corn
in August or in winter those of frozen sheaves.
Often he'd leave the Terraplane beside the highway
to enter the stunned silence of mid-September,
his eyes cast down for a sign, the only music
his own breath or the wind tracking slowly through
the stalks or riding above the barren ground. Later
he'd come home, his dress shoes coated with dust or mud,
his long black overcoat stained or tattered
at the hem, sit wordless in his favorite chair,
his necktie loosened, and stare at nothing. At first
my brothers and I tried conversation, questions
only he could answer: Why had he gone to war?
Where did he learn Arabic? Where was his father?
I remember none of this. I read it all later,
years later as an old man, a grandfather myself,
in a journal he left my mother with little drawings
of ruined barns and telephone poles receding
toward a future he never lived, aphorisms
from Montaigne, Juvenal, Voltaire, and perhaps a few
of his own: "He who looks for answers finds questions."
Three times he wrote, "I was meant to be someone else,"
and went on to describe the perfumes of the damp fields.
"It all starts with seeds," and a pencil drawing
of young apple trees he saw somewhere or else dreamed.

I inherited the book when I was almost seventy
and with it the need to return to who we were.
In the Detroit airport I rented a Taurus;
the woman at the counter was bored or crazy:
Did I want company? she asked, she knew every road
from here to Chicago. She had a slight accent,
Dutch or German, long black hair, and one frozen eye.

I considered but decided to go alone,
determined to find what he had never found.
Slowly the autumn morning warmed, flocks of starlings
rose above the vacant fields and blotted out the sun.
I drove on until I found the grove of apple trees
heavy with fruit, and left the car, the motor running,
beside a sagging fence, and entered his life
or my own for maybe the first time. A crow welcomed
me home, the sun rode above, austere and silent,
the early afternoon was cloudless, perfect.
When the crow dragged itself off to another world,
the shade deepened slowly in pools that darkened around
the trees; for a moment everything in sight stopped.
The wind hummed in my good ear, not words exactly,
not nonsense either, nor what I spoke to myself,
just the language creation once wakened to.
I took off my hat, a mistake in the presence
of my father's God, wiped my brow with what I had,
the back of my hand, and marveled at what was here,
nothing at all except the stubbornness of things.

NORTHERN MOTIVE

A modest house in a row of modest houses
in an ordinary neighborhood on the west side
of the city of Detroit. The year is 1949.
My older brother, back from the war, has moved on
with his bland wife into corporate America.
My mysterious brother, my twin, will marry
soon and open his own shop called Northern Motive
as though it explained the dreadful movies
about the royal Canadian Mounties. My mother
will decide she's at heart an entrepreneur
and open a dress shop in a desperate neighborhood
on Twelfth Street and slowly lose her savings, so slowly
that for years she'll believe for the first time
in the American dream. Long mornings I'm home
reading alone, though I burn with intensity
only in my night visions with the Victrola
spinning my personal recordings of Ravel,
who I regard as a genius second only to
Charlie Parker. What am I telling you?
That my origins are plain? That nothing explains
why one son out of three, a product of Central High,
not regarded as exceptional by others decides
he is chosen though no one else concurs.
No. That is too obvious. I have a motive,
though not a northern one. It involves flowers
growing on the median strip of the Outer Drive:
some called flags, purple, demure, silent even in wind;
little, delicate white jump-ups that open for
only a few hours, live their lives, and turn to dust
before the day ends; deep red poppies I won't see
for another twenty years along the hillsides
southwest of the town of Lorca as I head toward
the three holy cities of Andalusia,
a cheap hotel across from the railroad station,
a long night of fear for my wife and sons. To be poor
even in Spain is no reward. It was our life.
You build a life out of flags, poppies, branched twigs

found beside the road to Mijas, and you add gray stones
that deepen when spit on and reveal their natures,
bits of brown and green bark, a pinch of red earth
from the fields of La Mancha, a ray of sunlight
breaking through the clouds. As for music I had
the rail yards of Sevilla, the old one abandoned
now the town is rich. I had, too, the memory
of the great punch presses at Chevy, and Ravel
on scratchy 78s. And Charlie Parker
seated on a kitchen chair at the Flame Show Bar
between sets, a cigarette burning in one hand,
his eyes fixed on nothing. The closer you get
to things the more you see, the less you understand:
tiny spears of grass crossed in a pattern recalled
from a previous life, black ants by the hundred
scurrying back and forth in fear of my presence,
perhaps, or by a plan so old it's forgotten,
descending on foot into the Valley in July
knowing the river runs high in its banks, clear, cold,
born of last winter's snow waiting to be tasted,
waiting to heal the ache of our longings, waiting
even as it runs toward the sea to join our blood.
I'll call the river the Kings, as the locals do,
though its real name is Motive. It's only water,
what we washed our dishes in in 1949
after a dinner of Chinese take-out and Saltines
when business was good, and stacks of white Wonder Bread,
called "mattress stuffing," sandwiched around "horse cock"
or bologna by the precinct cops who served it to
the prisoners in the drunk tank on Sunday mornings
in the quiet world I left behind years ago
when I let the city burn. How ordinary
it all was, the dawn breaking each morning, dusk
arriving on time just as the lights of houses
came softly on. Why can't I ever let it go?

THE MERCY

The ship that took my mother to Ellis Island
eighty-three years ago was named "The Mercy."
She remembers trying to eat a banana
without first peeling it and seeing her first orange
in the hands of a young Scot, a seaman
who gave her a bite and wiped her mouth for her
with a red bandana and taught her the word,
"orange," saying it patiently over and over.
A long autumn voyage, the days darkening
with the black waters calming as night came on,
then nothing as far as her eyes could see and space
without limit rushing off to the corners
of creation. She prayed in Russian and Yiddish
to find her family in New York, prayers
unheard or misunderstood or perhaps ignored
by all the powers that swept the waves of darkness
before she woke, that kept "The Mercy" afloat
while smallpox raged among the passengers
and crew until the dead were buried at sea
with strange prayers in a tongue she could not fathom.
"The Mercy," I read on the yellowing pages of a book
I located in a windowless room of the library
on 42nd Street, sat thirty-one days
offshore in quarantine before the passengers
disembarked. There a story ends. Other ships
arrived, "Tancred" out of Glasgow, "The Neptune"
registered as Danish, "Umberto IV,"
the list goes on for pages, November gives
way to winter, the sea pounds this alien shore.
Italian miners from Piemonte dig
under towns in western Pennsylvania
only to rediscover the same nightmare
they left at home. A nine-year-old girl travels
all night by train with one suitcase and an orange.
She learns that mercy is something you can eat
again and again while the juice spills over
your chin, you can wipe it away with the back
of your hands and you can never get enough.

IV

THE SECRET

Somewhere the sea deepens
from blue to black, somewhere
a chemical dusk purples
the western sky, and the earth
sighs as it enters again
the old voyage toward morning.
In my backyard a square
marked by forget-me-nots,
lobelias, a lilac braced
in the aftermath of day.
The two surviving quail bark
from under the gnarled orange.
One month ago today
we dug your resting place
and dropped dust, dirt, ashes, no-
thing into the hole and bowed
under the full sun. You weren't
there as you're not in this haze,
nor in the first evening breeze.
You're not in the blackened loam
my wife prepared, nor in
the vast tent of sky stretched
above this valley, nor in
my words stumbling toward closure.
When you lived the secret
was yourself. You gave away
hours, days, years, 94 in all,
but never that. Your secret
is safe tonight. The earth turns
toward darkness, and the earth
asks nothing. The watching stars
shed what light they can, the moon
—with all its distant power—
rides out the darkness. Your sea,
a mountain range away, calmed,
enters a safe haven
that will last a single night.

The quail quiet at last. We
are one, sharing whatever
you are as blindness descends.

NOTES

PAGE 11   The Australian novelist referred to in "The Communist Party" is Helen Garner; the book she sent me was titled *True Stories*.

PAGE 12   The Clifford referred to in the title and the text of the poem is Clifford Brown, the great jazz trumpeter, who died at the age of twenty-five in an auto accident on June 26, 1956.

PAGE 26   "The Unknowable" owes everything to the life of Sonny Rollins.

PAGE 40   "Night Words" was inspired by the aphorisms of Juan Ramón Jimenez found in his book *The Complete Perfectionist*, edited and translated by Christopher Maurer.

PAGE 44   The title of "'He Would Never Use One Word Where None Would Do'" is taken from a description of Frankie Trumbauer by his widow.

PAGE 63   The title of "The Evening Turned Its Back Upon Her Voice" is an adaptation of a line by Mayakovsky.

PAGE 68   The poem "Cesare" was inspired by Cesare Pavese but is not based upon his life.

A NOTE ABOUT THE AUTHOR

Philip Levine was born in 1928 in Detroit and was formally educated there, at the public schools and at Wayne University (now Wayne State University). After a succession of industrial jobs he left the city for good and lived in various parts of the country before settling in Fresno, California, where he taught at the University until his retirement. He has received many awards for his books of poems, most recently the National Book Award in 1991 for *What Work Is,* and the Pulitzer Prize in 1995 for *The Simple Truth.*

A NOTE ON THE TYPE

This book is set in a typeface called Méridien, a classic roman designed by Adrian Frutiger for the French type foundry Deberny et Peignot in 1957. Adrian Frutiger was born in Interlaken, Switzerland, in 1928 and studied type design there and at the Kunstgewerbeschule in Zurich. In 1953 he moved to Paris, where he joined Deberny et Peignot as a member of the design staff. Méridien, as well as his other typeface of world reknown, Univers, was created for the Lumitype photoset machine.

Composition by NK Graphics, Keene, New Hampshire
Printed and bound by Edwards Brothers, Ann Arbor, Michigan
Designed by Harry Ford